BEA

Harry Thompson &
Marcus Berkmann

Illustrated by
Eddie McLachlan

CORGI BOOKS

BEARDIES

A CORGI BOOK   0 552 13048 6

First publication in Great Britain

PRINTING HISTORY

Corgi edition published 1986

Copyright © Harry Thompson & Marcus Berkmann 1986
Illustrations copyright © Edward McLachlan 1986

Acknowledgements to:
Michele Kimber, Gary Pritchard, Gordon Thompson and
Jean Berkmann Barwis

This book is set in 10/11pt Century Schoolbook

Corgi Books are published by Transworld Publishers Ltd.,
61-63 Uxbridge Road, Ealing, London W5 5SA, in Australia
Transworld Publishers (Aust.) Pty. Ltd., 15-23 Helles Avenue
Moorebank, NSW 2170, and in New Zealand by Transworld
Publishers (N.Z.) Ltd., Cnr. Moselle and Waipareira Avenues
Henderson, Auckland.

Printed and bound in Great Britain by
Cox & Wyman Ltd, Reading

BEARDIES or
THE BOOK OF THE BEARD

INTRODUCTION by JEAN-LUC BEARDY
of the Institut des Barbes, Paris

Hello, and a warm welcome to Beardies and non-Beardies alike.
You are reading THE BOOK OF THE BEARD.

As we know from the term 'Barbarian', the beard is an old-established feature of society dating back many hundreds of years at least. But could the beard be even older? Was the fabled city of Atlantis actually populated by a mysterious bearded civilization from under the sea? THE BOOK OF THE BEARD lifts aside the mystic veils of time and enables YOU to glimpse into the past.

Today the beard has metamorphosed and matured into a highly complex metaphor that charts the progress of society itself. Lenin and Karl Marx had beards. Queen Victoria didn't. Clearly, the significance of the beard as a social force is only beginning to dawn. The age of the beard is here.

THE BOOK OF THE BEARD is a major social document so explosive in content that it could well tear that society apart.

Jean-Luc Beardy
Institut des Barbes
Paris   1985

FOREWORD

By A Famous Bearded Bishop

Hullo. I'm a famous bearded bishop. You know, the other day, someone came up to me in the street and said, 'Hello. You're that famous bearded bishop, aren't you? Why did YOU grow a beard?' I paused for reflection, for my friend had indeed posed a knotty question. Why HAD I grown a beard?

Well, you know, the Bible tells us how Jehosophat once asked of St Bashevis, why did he throw the seedcorn unto the Hashemites? And St Bashevis replied, 'My son, go unto thine dwelling, and take thee an Oxen, and covet not the cousin of thy neighbour's wife if thee wishes to remain close to God'. And lo, Jehosophat went unto his neighbour's wife, and availed himself of her pigs instead. But Jehosophat had been impatient, and had disported himself upon the Sabbath day. And the Lord was unimpressed. And lo, a great plague smote down upon the land, and there were hailstones as great as cattle, and eggs as big as pumpkins, and newts as large as battleships, and all the people were utterly wiped out.

I think that satisfactorily answers the question, don't you? Suffice it to say that from that moment on, my friend's life became dedicated to the growing of a beard. And she's doing very well, thank you.

This book could put you on the same path. Sceptics may sneer, but the Lord in His Bearded Majesty may have other ideas. Amen.

©1985 A famous bearded bishop PLC

PS Can I have my cheque now?

FAMOUS PEOPLE WITH BEARDS

JESUS
GOD
SIR PETER HALL
CAPTAIN BIRDSEYE
LUCIFER
KING KONG
LENIN
PETER WITHE (Sheffield United)

FAMOUS PEOPLE WITHOUT BEARDS

GANDHI
DRACULA
THE POPE
MOTHER THERESA OF CALCUTTA
JAYNE MANSFIELD
IDI AMIN
KENNY SANSOM (Arsenal)

SOME PEOPLE WHO HAVE VERY SILLY BEARDS

FYFE ROBERTSON
The BHAGHWAN SHREE RAJNEESH
MIKE GATTING
ZZ TOP
THE DEVIL

FAMOUS PEOPLE NEARLY CALLED 'BEARD'

JOHN LOGIE BEARD
BRIGITTE BEARDOT
YOGI BEARD
MAX BEARDBOHM
THE BEARD OF AVON
THE BEARDROP EXPLODES (Pop Group)

THINGS TO DO WITH YOUR BEARD

A few holiday suggestions

Topiary

Beach Football

Sledging

Filling a mattress

Cleaning the floor

Disco Deadener

Joining the SDP

Weather-cheating

Suicide

7

WELL-KNOWN LIES ABOUT BEARDED PEOPLE

CONCERNED
INTELLIGENT
CARING
SENSITIVE
BEARD SIZE RELATED TO WILLY SIZE
NOT A MEMBER OF SDP/LIBERAL ALLIANCE

WELL-KNOWN TRUTHS ABOUT BEARDED PEOPLE

PIPE SMOKING
GUARDIAN READER
WEAK-CHINNED
HAIRY
EXTREMELY BORING

JOBS WHERE A BEARD IS NECESSARY

Ask your JOBCENTRE for more details
SDP CANDIDATE
OLD SEADOG
POLAR EXPLORER WITH A VERY LONG NAME
TV NATURALIST
GOD

ACTIVITIES WHERE A BEARD CAN BECOME A POSITIVE HINDRANCE

DRINKING SOUP
SHAVING
KISSING BABIES
ORAL SEX
LEAVING THE SDP/LIBERAL ALLIANCE
GYNAECOLOGY

ORGANIZATIONS YOU MAY CARE TO JOIN
That Promote Beard Welfare and Safety

BEARDPEACE
THE WORLD BEARDLIFE FUND
SAVE THE BEARD
RSPCB
FRIENDS OF THE BEARD
THE SDP/LIBERAL ALLIANCE

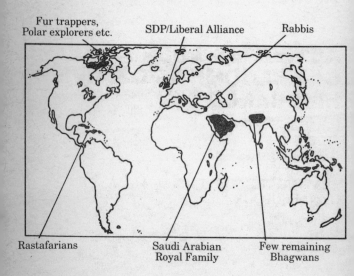

Fur trappers, Polar explorers etc.

SDP/Liberal Alliance

Rabbis

Rastafarians

Saudi Arabian Royal Family

Few remaining Bhagwans

BEARD DEMOGRAPHY
The Beard as endangered species: Provided by the World Beardlife Fund

SURVEY: Beard incidence in London & how to avoid Beards

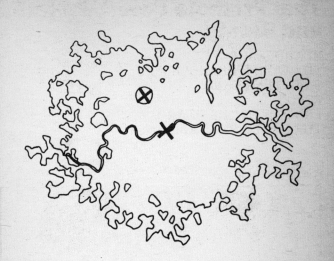

Avoid marked areas.

⊗   Hampstead

✕   Houses of Parliament

KNOW YOUR BEARDIE

The 'HERMIT' for
Destitutes

The 'VICAR' for
Whale-Savers

The 'ARTY FARTY' for
Old Bores

The 'SIR RANULPH' for
Polar Explorers & Old
Seadogs

The 'BEE GEE'
An M.O.R. beard useful in
advertising

The 'SCOTSMAN' for
Ethnics and other
undesirables

— BEARDS AT A GLANCE —

The 'SHEEPDOG' for
Hippies, Elderly Rock Stars
& Minor Deities

The 'SANTA CLAUS'
for Undercover
Store Detectives

Hullo

The 'CONCERNED' for
SDP Candidates

The 'PROFESSOR' for
Pseudo-Intellectuals & Oil
Sheikhs

The 'MORNING
AFTER . . .' for
Unemployables, Members of
the PLO and Bob Geldof

The 'COMPLETE IDIOT'
for Buffoons, Cretins &
Imbeciles

13 AMAZING FACTS YOU NEVER KNEW ABOUT BEARDS!

1) The children's game 'Beaver' consists of shouting 'Beaver' at bearded men in the street, pointing, laughing and running away.

2) The Russian Tsar Peter the Great put a tax on beards.

3) Egyptian Pharaohs were forced from an early age to wear false beards.

4) Sir Peter Hall has a beard.

5) Ostend's Chief of Police has forbidden his constables to sport beards in case members of the criminal fraternity set fire to them.

6) Such is Mrs Thatcher's hatred of beards that she refuses to appoint anyone with a beard to any Government post.

7) There are 13,000 hairs in the average beard.

8) According to *New Scientist* magazine, beard owners actually breathe in air that is not as fresh as everybody else's. Air they breathe out is partially trapped in their beards, and floats back up to be breathed in again.

9) 'Pogonaphobia' is a recognized psychiatric complaint meaning 'fear of beards'.

10) There are no bearded sitting MPs in the SDP.

11) The only non-bearded member of the pop group 'ZZ Top' is called 'Beard'.

12) M. Beard scored one goal for Birmingham City in the 1969–70 season.

13) The owner of the longest beard in the history of the world, Hans Steininger, fell to his death in 1567 when he tripped over it.

LET'S PARLER BEARD # 1

Just grown your first beard? Well, here are some phrases which will help you fit more easily into beardie society. Just memorize this list, then insert them, in the correct order, into the conversation at intervals.

'Mine's a pint of Thruxton's, Squire!'

'It's an exciting new centre party . . . a fresh dawn in British politics'

'Actually I'm working as a playwright at the moment . . . freelance . . .'

'Another pint of Thruxton's, if you will Squire, and one for yourself – as the Bishop said to the actress!'

'Mmmmm . . . it's what your right arm's for, eh Reg?'

'Yeah, we were all really stoned last Thursday, it was really amazing! Still, you've gotta laugh, 'aven't you eh Reg?'

'Keep on taking the pills Reg – ha ha ha'

'As I was saying . . . break the mould . . . single transferable vote . . . new system . . . another pint of Thruxton's luv, and seven packets of those new curried plum & ketchup crisps please'

'No, I was at Exeter University myself actually'

'I'll have another pint of your finest, darling. There's no answer to that, eh?'

'Actually I'm just starting a new play. The last one came back with some really encouraging and helpful comments on it'

'Shed a new light on democracy . . . consensus politics . . . middle way . . . hope for the future . . .'

' 'Scuse me a moment lads, I'm just off for a slash'

'Where's everybody gone?'

HOW TO TELL THE
A STYLE WARRIOR

Warlike damn-you eyes

Warlike hair style

Warlike lip-curl

Warlike dimple

Warlike lapel badge (NF etc)

Warlike Dior jacket

Warlike dazzling white trousers

Warlike car (BMW etc)

Warlike shoes

STYLE WARRIOR

DIFFERENCE BETWEEN
AND A BEARDIE

Recycled Bobble hat

Vacuous expression

Rucksack for Good Beer Guides, unusual beermats, beermugs, etc..

Concerned badges

Stained orange kagoule

Flared green corduroys

Leather-free shoes

Energy saving car Renault 4, 2CV or Metro

SHAVE THE WHALES

I ♥ TONY BENN

A HEDGEHOG IS A BRITAIN

BAN THE BOMB

CAMRA

O/S MAP

BEARDIE WARRIOR

A GLOSSARY OF BEARDSPEAK: WHAT THAT BEARDIE REALLY MEANS

IN THE PUB

To sink a pint ....Drink a pint of beer.

To down a jar ....Drink a pint of beer.

To swallow a jug ....Drink a pint of beer.

I'm really pissed...........................I'm slightly drunk.

God I'm pissed............I'm even more slightly drunk.

Jesus Christ, I'm absolutely
smashed out of my mind .. I'm moderately unsteady.

I had to be carried out
last night.......................I got the bus home last night.

I passed out ...... I cleaned my teeth and went to bed.

It's what your right arm's
for, Reg! ....I don't know what I'm talking about.

POLITICS

Committed .... Barmy.

Radical .... Barmy.

Embittered ....Unemployed.

Angry .... Still unemployed.

Thatcher's Britain .... Britain.

Exciting new centre party.............No one else would
have me.

Single transferable vote ....I lost my deposit
last time.

18

Impending breakthrough....No sign whatsoever of a
breakthrough.

Break the mould
of British politics ....I don't know what
I'm talking about.

SEX

My wife finds a beard attractive....She's got one too.
A beard shows strength in a man...............I've got a
weak chin.
My wife and I think that fidelity is no longer a
relevant concept....................She's having it off with
Mr Sadiq from the Newsagent's.
My wife likes hairy men ....Like that bastard
from the Newsagent's.
Besides, some men become more
attractive to women as they
get older ....I don't.
Anyway, you know what they say
about us beardies, eh?..No?
...You know, about beard size
being related to willy size ....I don't know what
I'm talking about.

HOW TO REMOVE

Some exciting new alternative methods

The Chomp Method

The Assissi Bird Lover Method

The Countryman or Annual Stubble Burning Method

The Kenwood Method

The Unravelling Method

The 'Ah-So' Method

YOUR BEARD

that you might care to try!

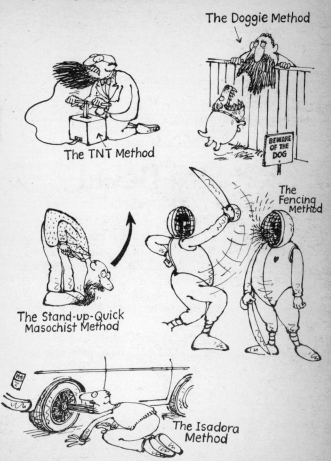

The Doggie Method

The TNT Method

The Fencing Method

The Stand-up-Quick Masochist Method

The Isadora Method

BEWARE OF THE DOG

THE BEARD IN SPORT

Few people realize just how versatile the human beard can prove in terms of sporting activity. Owning a beard opens up a whole new sporting vista for the Beardie to enjoy. Mornings and weekends, noon and night, any one of this wide variety of sports is ideally suitable for the bearded athlete.

FELLWALKING
AQUA FELLWALKING
TEN-PIN FELLWALKING
FORMULA ONE FELLWALKING
CROWN GREEN ORIENTEERING

Let's Parler Beard # 2

LESSON TWO OF OUR SERIES
'Good evening Officer'
'Just had a couple of jars with the lads officer . . . I'm on my way home actually'
'No fixed abode, Officer . . . I'm dossing at my friend Nav's place tonight'
'Er . . . a freelance playwright'
'Traffic cone? Oh, this traffic cone. Yes, I see what you mean'
'Er . . . shall I ride in the back?'
'By the way Officer, I feel I ought to inform you that I am a founder member of the SDP/Liberal alliance'

The Joy of Beard
– A Manual

1. STARTING OUT

In these days of carefree sex, heroin addiction, incest, bestiality, widespread necrophilia, sexually transmitted diseases and Keith Chegwin, life for a young couple can be difficult. Marital relations even more so.

But when a man and a woman come together, something beautiful and mysterious happens. Let us call this happening 'beard'. This is not something to be ashamed of. Nor can it be rushed into. Taken slowly, with due consideration for each other, 'beard' can be a moving experience: and before you know it, you will soon be in a position to experiment with other, more interesting and varied types of 'beard'.

2. TYPES OF 'BEARD' YOU MIGHT LIKE TO TRY

Oral Beard
Soixante-Beard
Group Beard
Beard-swapping
Beard with your dog
Beard with another bigger dog (watch the teeth)
Beard with the milkman
Beard while lashed to the radiator
Beard while buried up to your neck in sand
Beard from behind
Beard as a tax loss

Whatever you do decide to do with it, remember that what you have in your hand is a beautiful thing. Used properly, your beard could become an instrument of world peace and racial harmony.

THE BEARD IN HISTORY:

The History of the world from a beardie perspective

THE ANCIENT WORLD

The first real civilization grew up in the lands surrounding the Mediterranean and in the near east: the Babylonians, the Greeks, the Egyptians, the Persians and so on. But it was the Romans who surfaced as the most powerful nation in the ancient world. At this stage in the development of the world, the beard had little effect.

THE DARK AGES

By the fifth century AD, the Roman Empire had become complacent and so large as to be unwieldy: victory over all its enemies had lessened its will to fight. So it was that it became prone to a series of invasions by primitive, uncivilized tribes from the north and east. The Roman Empire fell prey to Huns, Goths, Vandals, Saxons, Franks, Visigoths, Lombards and so on. Some of these marauding tribes that had destroyed the Roman world wore beards, but apart from this the influence of the beard itself remained fairly minimal as yet.

THE MIDDLE AGES

Although still prone to turbulence, as seen in the expansionist activities of the Scandinavians and Arabs, the world was beginning to settle into new boundaries. The Europe that we know today was taking shape. The Mediterranean, however, remained the centre of power. At this stage the effect of beards remained tactical rather than strategic, that is to say barely discernible.

REFORMATION AND RENAISSANCE

For the first time the civilization known in the Roman world was surpassed, as the source of political power and cultural influence gradually spread north, away from the Mediterranean. The strong seafaring nations of the north-western seaboard, in many cases bolstered by newfound religious independence, branched out in the fields of trade and exploration. At this vital stage in global evolution, despite a high incidence of bearded seadogs in the new navies, the effect of beards on world history remained in abeyance. The age of the beard was yet to dawn.

THE INDUSTRIAL REVOLUTION

For the last two centuries, the world has been a vastly different place from that known to our predecessors, thanks to the influence of mechanization. The machine has brought with it mass production, mobility, communications, even flight, and with it mechanized warfare and all the awesome weapons of modern destruction. Standards of living boomed, democracy became a more popular form of government, and even communism came to the fore. At this stage the influence of the beard was still negligible.

THE FUTURE

Today, man is rushing ahead so fast that the future remains a mystery. What will come next? Computer beards? Digital beards? Will the microchip replace the beard? (No. Ed.) Only time will tell whether the beard will now go on to realize its full significance and build upon the groundwork laid so carefully over the centuries. We shall have to wait and see.

THE BEARD IN ART
BY A BEARDED ART CRITIC

R.I.B.A.*

Hullo. I'm a bearded art critic. And here are some of my favourite paintings, improved and enlivened – I'm sure you will agree – with a few delicately hirsute additions.

THE MONA LISA

Leonardo's simple, honest peasant-girl smile loses that homely, open-faced touch and takes on a sophisticated air of mystery when surrounded by an enigmatic shroud of beard. Suddenly an extra dimension is added to what had after all been only a simple sketch. What price the Mona Lisa now?

* ROYAL INSTITUTE OF BEARDED ARTISTS

DEJEUNER SUR L'HERBE

A masterpiece always flawed by its almost agoraphobic innocence, Manet's most celebrated work finally comes of age with a few subtly bearded brushstrokes. Gone are its naivete, its lack of sophistication. In their place, maturity, anticipation, variations of texture and beards.

THE HAYWAIN

Constable's historic vision of the English countryside has always been plagued by its lack of focus: all the beauties of Suffolk could not compensate for the absence of foreground. Now there is a focal point to concentrate the eye, and a lovely beard to look at instead of all those dull trees.

CHARACTER ANALYSIS THROUGH BEARDS

The Astonishing Facts

Now you too can get to know your beard by following the secret methods of the mystic east! The little-known art of 'Beardreading', adapted from ancient Samoan ritual practices, is a must for weddings, parties, and social occasions. Amaze your friends with your occult powers! Your new perception will enable YOU to interpret the subtlest changes of mood and manner which others will fail to notice! You need never be called a weakling again!!

Here are some of the secret 'beardpatterns' you must look for:

Joker

Long

Salesman

Aggressive

Weedy

CND

Feminist

Shy

Ill

Dead

Transplant

Bald

THE NATURAL WORLD OF THE BEARD

Wildlife in your beard; what you can grow.
'OLD FOOL' WRITES:

THE BEARDIE FARM

The human beard has been known to support a
surprisingly large range of animal life: simply keep
your beard damp and well-nourished, and depending
on its size it will be able to support anything from
algae up to small farm animals.
It's probably best to start with the easy stuff –
primitive vegetable matter, fungus and algae.
BROAD-LEAVED PONDWEED (potamogeton
natans) is a good starter, and a few sprigs of WATER
PLANTAIN (Alisma plantago-aquatica) will add
colour and variety to your beard.
At this stage it should be possible to introduce simple
animal life in the shape of LICE (Anoplura)
EARWIGS (Dermaptera) and COCKROACHES
(Orthoptera family) and then the rodents that feed on
them. DORMICE (Muscardinus avellanarius) will
sleep quietly in a beard, or for those wishing to be
particularly discreet the HAIRY-ARMED BAT
(Nyctalus leisleri) will hang fairly inconspicuously at
the back. However the common STOAT (Mustela
erminea) can be a difficult predator to harbour.
Birds, too, can be encouraged to nest in thicker
beards, and the engaging twitter of birdsong is a
pleasant alternative to the harsh noise of an alarm
clock on those sunny spring mornings. Anything up to
the size of a rook is to be encouraged, but you must
beware of harbouring any bird large enough to want

to remove its nest to another location should the need arise.

At this point it is worth thinking in terms of using your beard for commercial purposes – as a BEARDIE FARM. Ordinary farm animals, egg-laying fowl and even small pigs will live comfortably in a sufficiently sizeable beard: or why not try fur farming? The MINK (Mustela vision) is a profitable if problematic beard guest.

Flowers are another element that will bring life and colour to a drab, lifeless beard while earning a little extra money on the side. Hydrangeas and Nasturtiums are perennial favourites, but are too commonly available. The artful Beardie will make use of the special conditions prevailing in his beard to grow wild flowers – climbers like HONEYSUCKLE (Lonicera periclymenum) in the thick of the beard and GENTIAN (Gentiana asclepiadea) or SEA PINK (Armeria Maritima) on the exposed upper slopes.

Your beard will also, of course, support MARIJUANA – amongst other things! But beware – you don't want your beard to be busted. Be especially careful if one of the pigs living in your beard is an undercover pig from the drug squad: it's the suppliers that get hit hardest.

Good growing!

BEARD MAINTENANCE
How to clean your Beard: Some methods and their drawbacks

METHOD *1
THE AUTOMATIC CAR WASH.
1. Drive into an automatic car wash.
2. Leave the window open.
3. Hey Presto! Your beard has
   been cleaned!
This method is also useful if
there is anything else you want
cleaned, but it can be rather indiscriminate.

METHOD *2
METHYLATED SPIRITS
1. Soak an old rag in methylated spirits.
2. Rub your beard down with it.
This method is not recommended for
pipe-smokers.

METHOD *3
THE WASHING MACHINE
1. Set the washing machine to 'fast coloureds'
   pour in powder and conditioner.
2. Cut your beard off.
3. Put it in the washing machine,
   close the door and switch on.

Warning:
This method can be problematic if
you wish to use the beard again.

BEARDIE RECIPES

BEARDIE RECIPES ARE CHEAP, FUN TO MAKE
AND ECOLOGICALLY SOUND! BY RECYCLING
THE WASTE FOOD LEFT IN YOUR BEARD AFTER
PREVIOUS MEALS, YOU CAN MAKE DELICIOUS
ORGANIC AND MACROBIOTIC FOOD FOR ANY
OCCASION!

What to squeeze out of your beard
BOUILLABEARDDE

Grease a bowl and crack 2 eggs into it. Then add:
    ¼ pint milk
    Pinch salt
    1pt chicken stock
    1 tsp tarragon
Bring to the boil and wring the contents of your beard
into it.
Then strain and simmer for 70 minutes.
The strained lumps can then be spread onto bread or
used as garnish.

SOME OTHER DISHES YOU
MAY CARE TO MAKE
Beard Bourguignon
Beard Strogonoff
Beard's Nest Soup
Beardburgers
Shredded Beard (with milk)

THE BEARD IN ROCK – AN EXPOSITION
by CHRIS GOSH

Chris Gosh was born in 1951 and is a lecturer in Applied Reggae at Wolverhampton Polytechnic. He is the author of 'Social Comment and Polyphony: Techniques in Struggle' (1978).

'Rock music, that corrupt interface of rhythm and emotion, has throughout its three decade evolution closely mirrored crucial developments in the field of facial hair. The beard, that astute tangle of manhood and war, that furry matrix of nature untamed, has in the rich tapestry of pop accounted for many a vital stitch. Beard as Trotskyite statement. Beard as psychological mask. Beard as glorification of machismo. Each is an entirely valid stance. And it's no coincidence that some of the most revolutionary figures of rock have spurned the razor:

A. ROGER WHITTAKER. As a leader of the 'whistling underground' of the late sixties, Whittaker rejected bourgeois instrumentation for a closer relationship with the ultimate musical accompaniment, his mouth. This primal minimalism soon projected him to the acclaim of the avant garde, and although derided by the fanatical clean-shaven establishment, many of Whittaker's grooves stand today as bearded classics.

B. 'MR' ACKER BILK. In 1964 the world watched Merseybeat, but it was in the seedy jazz clubs of Bournemouth and Chelmsford that a more significant revolution was taking place, one that was to push back the parameters of musicalization. It is no secret in rock circles that the Beatles grew their short-lived beards only after a profound experience at a Bilk gig.

C. ROLF HARRIS. Another great musical pathfinder, with his pioneering exponency of the didgerydoo, and his searing critique of pederasty, 'Two Little Boys'. Now, though, years after his peak, the forces of Beardist prejudice compel Harris to work as a lonely media personality presenting old cartoons for TV: a tragic waste of a brilliant career.'

©Chris Gosh.

FOR FURTHER REFERENCE
Vital bearded works include:

Demis Roussos/HAPPY TO BE ON AN ISLAND IN THE SUN (1975) Philips 6042 033

Classic zebra in the annals of punkadelia. Roussos' sparse phrasing contrasts vividly with the rasped riffing of Yannis Stassinopoulos' guitar to produce a seminal work of pre-punk modernism.

Roger Whittaker/THE LAST FAREWELL (1975) EMI 2294

Producer Norrie Paramour's driving backbeat overlaid with Whittaker's taut rapping predated such of today's important bands as Interesting Observations from a Train, Liquid Assassins and Morality in Housework, though it is not known to have influenced any of them whatsoever.

Adrian Gurvitz/CLASSIC (1982) RAK 339

'I'm living in an attic,' wrote Gurvitz, encapsulating in lyric the aspirations of a generation bereft of hope. His darkly menacing vocals, sparingly applied, come straight from the beard.

Brian & Michael/MATCHSTALK MEN AND
MATCHSTICK CATS AND DOGS (1978)
Pye 7N 46035

Since neglected masterpiece of the genre. B & M's
acoustic guitars thrust and parry in a committed
duello that forms a savage indictment of Lowry's
patrician disdain for the ordinary working man, cat
and dog (or woman, cat and dog). 12" dub version
particularly recommended.

'Mr' Acker Bilk with the Leon Young String Chorale/
STRANGER ON THE SHORE (1961) Columbia D8
4750

The pounding snarework of skinsman Duggie Sprot
provides the foundation for a slice of vintage Bilk in
this his *Meisterwerk*. Bilk's powerhouse vocals and
richly upholstered funk trumpetry emphasize his
lucid *Weltanschauung* and unambiguous *Zeitgeist*. As
Goethe put it, 'Es irrt der Mensch, so lang er strebt'.

Let's Parler Beard # 3

LESSON THREE IN OUR FASCINATING COURSE

'I swear to tell the truth, the whole truth and nothing
but the truth'
'A freelance playwright, M'lud'

'Yes M'lud, I do. This is a clear case of police
harrassment. The nine Officers in question behaved in
a manner which I can only describe as frankly
beardist. The last 24 hours, M'lud, have been nothing
short of an Orwellian nightmare, M'lud'

'Er . . . can I have a week to find the money?'

INSTANT BEARD

A cut-out and colour false beard for the whole family to enjoy.

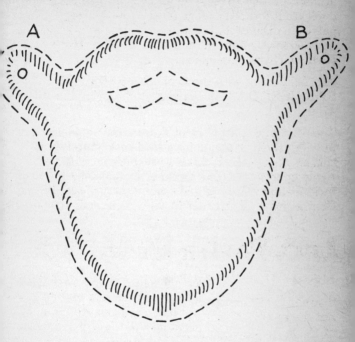

1. Cut along the dotted line.
2. Pierce holes at A and B and tie string through each hole.
3. Adjust length of string to fit.
4. Attach the false beard to your face. Fool your friends and influence people!

THE BEARD ENIGMA

In these days of rational scientific thinking, few enigmas are more puzzling to the modern scientist than the enigma of the Beard. Where do beards come from? How did they originate? PROFESSOR ERICH VON BEARDIKEN charts some of the more famous beard enigmas and comes up with some startling theories.

CHARIOTS OF THE BEARDS

On the plain of Nazca in the Peruvian highlands, huge lines, both curved and straight, have been carved out of the earth. Could these lines represent the fragments of giant beards, drawn in homage to an astral civilization of giant bearded gods? Surely it is more than a coincidence that the majority of today's ancient deities are depicted wearing beards? Did 'the bearded ones' really come from another planet? Will we ever know?

THE BEARDMUDA TRIANGLE

Off the eastern seaboard of the southern United States is an apparently commonplace area of sea into which scores of ships, boats and aircraft have disappeared without trace. This fateful area is shaped in a triangle – exactly the same shape as a human beard. Could this be more than a coincidence? Is it connected with the ancient underwater civilization of bearded folk, the fabled 'Beardlantians', who with their sweet singing and fishy tails have lured countless generations of seamen to their doom? Is it any coincidence that the name 'Bermuda' contains the letters B-E-A-R-D?

BEARDHENGE

In the misty fastness of Salisbury plain lies the site of

'Beardhenge', one of the most enduring enigmas of the megalithic age. Here was a circle of beards, ritually cut from their owners and laid in a ring by the Druids of the ancient folk. Was this mere religious ritual? Or did the beards represent a giant computer? Unfortunately all trace of the beards has disappeared so we will never know.

THE BEARDIE CELESTE

In the middle of the last century, a French barque came across a ship, unmanned and deserted, floating in the open sea. Everything was left as if life had been interrupted by a sudden cataclysm. The table was set for dinner, meals uneaten. Books were left unread, half-opened. And most curiously of all, the crew had left behind all their shaving equipment. Wherever they had disappeared to, it was certain that they would all by now have very long beards.

THE SDP/LIBERAL ALLIANCE

Back in the middle of 1981, a group of politicians announced that they were forming a new party, to 'break the mould' of British politics. Quickly they chose 'Fanfare for the Common Man' as their campaigning music. The sound of this music spread across the land, across the fields and across the towns, and into people's homes: and as soon as they heard it, all the bearded people everywhere stopped what they were doing to listen. Then, one by one, they put down their *Guardians*, their pipes and their pints of real ale and began to walk towards the sound of the music as if mesmerized. The throng grew and grew as more and more beardies began to join, and as it grew so the beardies started to dance. And they danced over the hill and down dale until they had completely disappeared out of sight. And amazing as it may seem, neither they nor the new party were ever heard of again.

THE BEARD IN LITERATURE — A competition

The beard has always had a fond place in the hearts of British literature-lovers. All *you* have to do is match the beard to the poetry or prose: so if you think piece 1 was written by beard A, then enter an A in the box opposite the 1. But there's a catch: the identities of the beards' owners are not revealed!

PIECE 1
When shall we three meet again
In thunder, lightning or in rain?
When the hurlyburly's done,
When the battle's lost and won.

PIECE 2
What men or gods are these? What maidens loth?
What mad pursuit? What struggle to escape?
What pipes and timbrels? What wild ecstasy?

PIECE 3
She was silently weeping, and he lay with her
and went into her there on the hearthrug, and
so they gained a measure of equanimity.

PIECE 4
Fog everywhere. Fog up the river, where it
flows among green aits and meadows; fog down
the river, where it rolls defiled among the
tiers of shipping, and the waterside pollutions
of a great (and dirty) city.

BEARD A   BEARD B   BEARD C   BEARD D

I think that piece   was written by beard

| 1 |
| 2 |
| 3 |
| 4 |

WORLDS WITHIN BEARDS
A look through the microscope

Beardowners of a nervous disposition may prefer to skip these next few pages, as the Book of the Beard turns the spotlight on the fantastic microscopic world of the beard, and some of the weird and wonderful creatures that teem and multiply beneath our very mouths. The common beardtick, the hirsute louse and the stray toupee mite are common visitors to our chins, but the all-seeing camera of master lensman Kurt Baldheim (of the Berlin Bardfotografieinstitut) has captured some of the more exotic fauna to grace the nation's whiskers.

For instance, the rarely seen mile-long Beardworm, or the fabulous Gatting's beardhopper, which can eat up to 900 times its own bodyweight in barbiverous solids every hour. Or there is the wondrous chameleon-like Whittaker's Beardmoth, which can assume the shape, size, hue and odour of any human beard, as well as the political viewpoint of its owner, while sitting motionless for weeks on the bleakest of chinscapes.

OTHER SPECIES YOU MIGHT LIKE TO TRY:
Anti-racist Maggot
Single Transferable Ant
Nuclear-free Millipede

HOW BEARDS GROW
But the cameras of Dr Baldheim take us even further into this microscopic world, beyond the ticks, flukes and other parasites nesting between the hairs, down to the very origins of beard life itself. Now, for the first time, using an electron microscope, Dr Baldheim

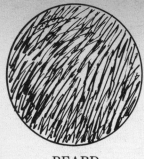

BEARD
(detail)

HALL'S BEARDWEEVIL
(twice actual size)

**GATTING'S
BEARDHOPPER**
(actual size)

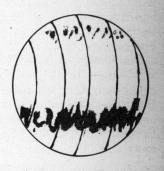

**MILE-LONG
BEARDWORM**
(detail)

can reveal that the beard is not as was previously
thought a bodily function, harking back to a primitive
biological need for warmth and protection, but is in
fact itself a *cellular parasite*, feeding off the
nourishment in the human chin. Just look at the
extraordinary set of illustrations overleaf.

1. Clean shaven cells sit happily in a barren chinscape. There are no worries on the horizon.

2. A lone bearded cell appears, but the unsuspecting clean shaven cells as yet remain unperturbed.

3. Suddenly the invader starts to multiply.

4. The clean shaven cells attempt to reproduce in turn, but the bearded cells are too quick for them.

5. The massacre is all over within a few minutes. Only a razor can save us now.

PUMPING BEARD!

The MAN'S way to fitness and health!

TIRED of having sand kicked in your beard?
TIRED of beautiful girls laughing at your puny whiskers?
TIRED of repeatedly being rejected by the SDP/Liberal Alliance?

NOW people will look your beard in the face again and QUAKE.

PUMPING BEARD is a revolutionary new fitness technique that channels the body's muscular energy DIRECTLY to the follicles, stimulating hair growth and turning YOUR beard into a potentially devastating weapon if used correctly. The 'PUMPING BEARD' method has been specially devised for your benefit by internationally renowned expert Dr Bengt Korkscrew, of Stockholm's famous Beardhuset.

BEFORE

AFTER

CLUB BEARDIE

ACTION-PACKED HOLIDAYS FOR THE CONSCIENCE-STRICKEN

'FAR FROM THE MADDING CROWD'
No Beardie likes to be cooped up on a boring old package tour in just another purpose-built resort! Now CLUB BEARDIE has devised the perfect tour schedule for the discerning Beardie: holidays where YOU come face to face with the world's problems and can actually HELP. No more lemonade and chips on the Costa Brava! Now you can finally ABSOLVE YOUR GUILT in a very real sense!

1. AFGHAN RAMBLE
   Two months caught in the crossfire in subzero temperatures in the scenic mountain pass of El-Imminent-Doth. Your chance to act as arbitrator – make the Russians and the rebels shake hands and patch up the whole silly quarrel. Includes free ride in a helicopter gunship back to Kabul for interrogation.

2. KAMPUCHEAN JUNGLE TREK
   A thrilling and scenic break amongst the blazing rice paddies of South East Asia. Your chance to help administer basic necessities (food, blankets, medical help, Space Invaders) to the children of the 'Killing Fields' under a constant barrage of napalm.

3. PERSIAN GULF CRUISE
   'Water, water, everywhere, and not a drop to drink' – yes – Coleridge Taylor's famous lines actually come true on our three week 'Gulf Gauntlet' Trip,

culminating in an outing to the disease-ridden marshlands of the battlefront at Basra. Find out the truth about the Exocet's capabilities – YOUR chance to become the next Tam Dalyell. (All bunks shared with 113 Taiwanese merchant seamen).

4. BEIRUT PUB CRAWL

A stroll around the waterholes of East and West Beirut with our experienced tour guide Yogurtlu Kebab: sample the ales of the middle east in an atmosphere of real comfort. (Hotel accommodation subject to continuing existence of hotel).

QUIZ – Have YOU got a beard?

If you haven't got a mirror, here's an easy way to find out.

1) Do you shave regularly?
   A–Yes B–No
2) Do babies burst into tears when you kiss them?
   A–No B–Yes
3) Do you read *The Guardian* for any reason other than the job adverts?
   A–No B–Yes
4) Are you a member of the SDP/Liberal Alliance?
   A–No B–Yes

If you answered 'A' to all these questions, then you haven't got a beard. If you answered 'B' to all these questions, you probably do. If not, seek medical advice at once.

THE BEARDIE CONQUEST OF SPACE

BY A BEARDED SCIENTIST

Hello, I'm a bearded scientist. You know, as I look around me, I notice that the age of space travel is now upon us, and I can't help thinking about how only thirty years ago they laughed at Jules Verne when he foresaw the technology that would one day enable bearded astronauts to bridge the mighty voids of space. Even more recently, they scorned H.G. Wells, when he predicted a means of travel which would one day launch men with beards across the cosmic gulf to the stars.

Although no-one with a beard has actually yet been on a spacecraft, already scores of films have shown bearded space pilots being shot down by scaly green intergalactic life.

CLOSE ENCOUNTERS OF THE BEARDED KIND

Scientists now believe that the possibility of other intelligent life forms existing somewhere in the galaxy is 1:83 billion. By the same token, the probability of discovering an intelligent bearded life form is not far behind. Somewhere out there (points at window) could be a race of Super-Beardies who have attained a cultural and intellectual perfection: righting wrongs, voting for the Mega-Alliance, promoting the cause of minority planets, drinking hyper-ale and saving gay whales. It can only be a matter of time before entire shiploads of these beardies descend upon our planet, bearing peace, goodwill and underarm smells.

1. Fasten helmet & straps.

2. Take off.

3. Attain maximum speed of 7,000,000,000mph.

4. Catch sight of alien in rear view mirror.

5. Announce, "I can't hold her- she's breaking up!"

6. Shout " Aaaaargh!"

THE FUTURE

So what does the future hold for this bewhiskered island race? Will we one day metamorphose into another stage of our development, as intergalactic beardies? (No. Ed.) Who can really tell?

©1985 A Bearded Scientist

FUN AND GAMES WITH BEARDS!

SOME PUZZLES & BRAIN-TEASERS TO TEST
YOUR IMAGINATION Set by 'Uncle Crappy'.
Answers at foot of page.

1) Q: Can you reunite Sir Edgar with his lost beard?

2) Q: Oliver, Rolf & Jeremy all want to grow a beard – but only one of them can. Can you tell which one?

3) Q: If Sally has six beards, Denzil has three beards and Sir Peter has none, Sally divides her beards equally between the three of them and Denzil then gives one fifth of his beards each to the other two, who has the most beards?

4) Q: Can you make the word 'beard' by moving only two matches?

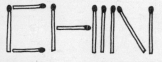

THE BEARD IN ASTROLOGY

A Beardie re-interpretation

'Cassandra' writes: The ancient science of astrology is broadly divided into two schools, the Chinese and Western forms of Astrology. But few know of a mysterious third form of Astrology, considered by

CAPRICORN   PISCES   AQUARIUS

ARIES   TAURUS   GEMINI

some to be even older: the so called 'Beardie scrolls'.
Now Astrologers believe that the twelve signs of the
zodiac can be re-interpreted. The constellations
themselves seem to acquiesce in the Beardie scheme.

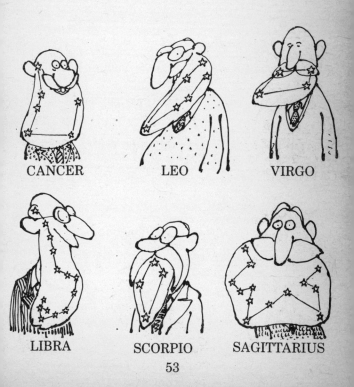

CANCER LEO VIRGO

LIBRA SCORPIO SAGITTARIUS

ARE YOU A REAL BEARDIE?

YOU MAY HAVE A BEARD – BUT ARE YOU A
BONA-FIDE BEARDIE?
FIND OUT FROM OUR FUN-TO-ANSWER QUIZ,
PROVIDED BY THE CAMPAIGN
FOR REAL BEARDS, AND YOU COULD WIN
YOURSELF A SUPER CASH PRIZE!

1. Which of the following publications is your
   favourite?
   a) Just Seventeen
   b) Christian Science Monitor
   c) The Guardian
   d) What Micro?
   e) What Beard?

2. Which of the following drinks is your favourite?
   a) Babycham
   b) Slalom Lager, in the exciting new 500 ml bottle
   c) Emva cream Cyprus sherry
   d) Water
   e) Mine's a pint of Thruxton's, Squire!

3. What job do you do?
   a) Page 3 Girl
   b) Chief of Nato
   c) Both of the above
   d) Assistant Bank Manager
   e) Polar explorer with a very long name

4. Which of these is your favourite TV programme?
   a) Terry and June
   b) Good Morning Britain
   c) The Price is Right
   d) Naya Vengsarkar Zengi Vindaloo (Channel
      Four's adventurous new magazine for the
      Hindustani community)
   e) Party political broadcast on behalf of the SDP/

Liberal Alliance
5. Who is your favourite media personality?
   a) Nicholas Parsons
   b) Samantha Fox
   c) The Bhaghwan Shree Rajneesh
   d) David Bellamy
   e) Sir Peter Hall
6. Who would be your ideal sex partner?
   a) Victoria Principal
   b) Bo Derek
   c) Joan Collins
   d) Felicity Kendal
   e) Clement Freud (SDP/Liberal Alliance)

HOW DID YOU RATE?
A Bearded Doctor Writes:
SCORE 1 point for every (a) answer, 2 for every (b) and so on.

6–13 FILAMENTOUS
   Sorry, chum – that's no beard, that's bumfluff. Get cracking on the Thruxton's!

14–20 CRINITE
   Improving – but still little better than five o'clock shadow. Why not enrol in a polar expedition?

21–27 HISPID
   Not bad! You could probably use it in lieu of a brillo pad, but it's still not a man's beard. Try a life subscription to the New Statesman, or get a job in a wholefood restaurant.

28–30 SODDING HAIRY
   Great! You're a real beardie. Not just physically bearded, but spiritually bearded. Don't forget to renew your subscription to CAMRA!

BEARD MART

A SELECTION OF PRODUCTS FOR THE
DISCERNING BEARDIE

BEARD COSMETICS

Keep your beard looking youthful, with our extensive
range of beauty and maintenance products.

CACHAREL POUR BARBE
A subtle eau-de-toilette to enhance the ambience of
your beard. Comes in three flavours – strawberry,
chocolate, and duck a l'orange.

KOREAN BEARD GINSENG
Keep your beard looking
youthful and alert with this age-
old potion of the mystic east,
culled from the phlegmy
secretions of the Asiatic swamp
hog.

NEW BEARDOL
Make your natural beardcolour a shade more boring.
Try our exciting new colour range (Khaki, Puce).

THERMAL BEARDWARMER

Remarkable new solar-powered technology keeps your beard snug and cosy. Simply attach adaptor to the roof of your house. Comes complete with 500 yards of flex FREE. Made in Taiwan.

BEARD-O-LARM

Does YOUR beard catch fire when connected up to unsafe Taiwanese heating appliances? This new pocket-size beard alarm is connected directly to New Scotland Yard! At the first whiff of smoke a fleet of patrol cars will be at your doorstep within the week. Made in Taiwan.

Comes complete with matching stereo accessories, including whistle, buzzer or American police siren (as seen on TV's Starsky and Hutch).

Is YOUR beard going bald? Spare your blushes with this fabulous lifelike

BEARD TOUPEE

in real otter hair. You need never be a bald beardie in public again.

Comes in: Curly.Shaggy.Straggly.Smelly. PLUS Free can of Otter Repellant.

BEARDDISSOLVE

Is YOUR beard getting you down? Rid yourself of that unwanted facial growth with new BEARDDISSOLVE©– The all-in-one beard remover!

Your BEARDDISSOLVE® kit comes complete in six exciting parts:
1) Instruction leaflet (in seven languages)
2) Hygienic klingfilm wrap
3) Attractive cardboard mount
4) Free membership opportunity to join the BEARDDISSOLVE club
5) Box
6) Breadknife

BEFORE   AFTER

Also Available:
Home plastic surgery and junior lung bypass kit.

ALL PRODUCTS NOW AVAILABLE FROM 'JUST BEARDS', OF CHALK FARM, LONDON NW1.

Beardokleen

Tired of those unmentionable beardstains? Fed up of seeing your whiskers gummed up with sticky substances? Lost another unfinished Anglo Bubbly in there somewhere? Now those days are gone!
New lemon fresh BEARDOKLEEN will rid your beard of unwanted bacteria, sweat, tobacco, baked beans, soup, small furry animals, old copies of 'Sanity', and so on.

Available in hundreds of exciting shades! (Khaki & Puce)

HEATED BEARD ROLLERS

Say bye-bye to those shaggy beard blues!

BEFORE   AFTER

Get YOUR beard a-swirlin' an' a-curlin' with these new steam-driven heated beard rollers!
(As used by Mike Gatting, Middlesex CC and England Test Star).

LUM-O-BEARD

Now you will never lose your way in the dark again.
New 'Lum-o-beard' portable beardlight fits
inconspicuously into the sparsest beard.
Completely undetectable.

FLYING BEARDS

BORED of those bare walls? CAN'T afford a picture?
LOOK NO FURTHER! Join the jet set with these new
'Flying Beard' wall decorations. Tasteful flying beards
will enliven your surroundings and provide a talking
point. Only £399.00. As used by Sir Peter Hall.

Trivial Hirsute™

Buy new TRIVIAL HIRSUTE!
The amazing general knowledge beard game.

250,000,000 questions and answers on every aspect of beard life.

Questions fall into one amazing category: BEARDS. This game comes to you at the amazingly trivial price of only £799,000,000,000,000,000,000,000 (box & pieces extra).

Is your beard sluggish on those cold mornings? Up to 95% of all body heat is lost through the beard, so why not buy a lovely HAND-CROTCHETED BEARDCOVER!

Protect YOUR beard against frost, hail, beardbugs and termites.
Made from real simulated beardthreads in glowing colour.
Don't delay – get it today!

BEARDS IN THE PRESS

The controversy continues

ANGUS D̶ ̶ ̶ ̶ ̶ ̶ ̶ ̶

Chairman, Railway Conversion League,
Chertsey, Surrey.

No complaints

SIR—What damned impertinence from Mrs R. Dorothy Cole (Dec. 28) about the banning of beards.

I have worn a beard for at least 25 years and have never had cause for complaint from anyone.

I strongly resent the inference that any man who wears a beard also wears casual clothes and is sloppy in his behaviour.

I would resent any firm for which I worked ordering me to shave off my beard. I would consider it an intrusion on my civil liberties and they could keep their job.

R. H. WHEATLEY
London, S.W.15.

BARBLIOGRAPHY

A selection of further bearded reading.

A History of the Corduroy Trouser, by Montagu
Goblin (Hedgerow Press, 1973)
A Future That Will Work, by Dr David Owen (Viking,
1984)
Jeremy Beadle's Book of Money (Money Press, 1985)
Atomic Rooster: the Formative Years, by Kaz Kagoule
(Armpit Press, 1978)
Youth Hostelling for the Disabled, by Olly Thruxton
(Dullard & Dullard, 1975) illus. by the author
Both Poles in a Weekend, by Sir Rodolph Cheate
(Airlift Press, 1980)
Face the Future, by Dr David Owen (Penguin, 1981)
Up Everest by Tongue, by Sir Rodolph Cheate (Fraud
Books, 1982)
The Bhopal Disaster: It Could Happen Here, by Waz
Flysheet (Real Ale Books, 1985)
The Pipe in Rural England 1324–27, by Denzil Fart
PhD (Staffs. Poly imprint, 1962)
The Vanishing World of the Salamander, by Baz Toad
(Toad Press, 1976)
A Unified Health Service, by Dr David Owen (1968)
It's because my beard was there, by Sir Rodolph
Cheate (Runner-up Press, 1986)

Who knows, perhaps these few diverse strands of
bearded knowledge could yet grow and coalesce, to
become the future key to humankind's destiny, and
those sorts of things.

Let's Parler Beard # 4

LESSON FOUR IN OUR BEARDIE
UNDERSTANDING SERIES

'Long time no see, Reg! I'll have the usual please'

'Y'know Reg – the usual . . . a pint of Thruxton's. Oh, and some of those new strawberry and salamander crisps'

'I've had a short holiday Squire . . . er . . . walking in the Mendips actually . . . needed inspiration for the new play. It's going to be about prison reform'

'Another pint of your best, please, mine host! It's a long time since I've had a jar . . . that is to say . . . er . . .'

'I'm off for a slash'